Nature's Children

SNAILS

Jen Green

GROLIER

FACTS IN BRIEF

Classification of Snails

Phylum: *Mollusca* (mollusks)

Class: *Gastropoda* (gastropods)

Species: Over 50,000 species. There are two subclasses of snails with gills, *Prosobranchi* and *Opisthobranchia*, and one subclass of snails with lungs, *Pulmonata*.

World distribution.   Worldwide except Arctic and Antarctic. Most in tropical regions.

Habitat.   On land in mainly moist places, including forests and grasslands. Also widespread in fresh and salt water.

Distinctive physical characteristics.   Smallish, soft-bodied creatures protected by a hard shell. Soft body sticks out of the shell and has head with tentacles and muscular foot.

Habits.   These slow-moving animals are active at night and after rain. They hibernate during cold weather or drought.

Diet.   Mainly plants, but also animal remains, dung, and fungi. Some species are parasites or predators that catch live prey.

© 2004 The Brown Reference Group plc
Printed and bound in U.S.A.
Edited by John Farndon and Angela Koo

Published by:

GROLIER

**An imprint of Scholastic
Library Publishing
Old Sherman Turnpike, Danbury,
Connecticut 06816**

Library of Congress Cataloging-in-Publication Data
Green, Jen.
   Snails / Jen Green.
     p. cm. — (Nature's children)
   Includes index.
   Summary: Describes the physical characteristics, habits, and natural environment of snails.
   ISBN 0–7172–5957–9 (set)   ISBN 0–7172–5973–0
    1. Snails—Juvenile literature. [1. Snails.] I. Title. II. Series.

QL430.4.G74 2004
594'.3—dc22

2003049177

Contents

What little creature can crawl without legs? Has a foot but no toes? Carries its home on its back? The answer is a snail. Snails and their close relatives slugs belong to a group of animals called mollusks. Both slugs and snails have soft, slimy bodies, but only snails have shells. Snails, slugs, winkles, and limpets make up a group of mollusks called gastropods. This word means "stomach-foot." These little creatures seem to creep along on their stomachs, but in fact they glide on a broad, flat foot.

The world of snails holds many surprises. We think of slugs and snails as slow, but in fact some are quite speedy. Snails are also amazingly strong—they can lift many times their own weight. Some snails have lived for many years. Snails thought to be long dead have woken up and come back to life!

Opposite page: About 4 inches (11 centimeters) long, the Roman snail is the biggest snail in Europe. This is the snail the French eat, and it has become very rare in the wild.

All in the Family

As well as slugs and snails, the mollusk group contains a variety of other creatures. Clams, scallops, oysters, mussels, squids, and octopuses are all mollusks. The various mollusks can look quite different, but they all have soft bodies. Many have shells, too.

The giant clam, weighing up to 550 pounds (250 kilograms), is the heaviest mollusk. The giant squid is the biggest. Oysters are famous for making beautiful pearls if a piece of grit gets into their shells. The oyster surrounds the grit with a shelly layer to prevent damage to its soft body. This builds up to form a pearl.

Squid, octopus, and their relatives cuttlefish are intelligent, active mollusks. These sea creatures have many arms. They swim along by squirting a jet of water through a rubbery tube or funnel on their foot. These mollusks have the amazing ability to change the color of their skin in seconds. They do this to hide from their enemies and also to express their feelings to their pals!

Like snails, this broadclub cuttlefish is a mollusk.
It lives in the Pacific Ocean around Australasia.

The World of Snails

There are many types of snails beside the common snails that creep around your garden. You may be surprised to hear that there are over 50,000 species (types) of snails around the world! Some have dull-colored shells. Others are brightly colored. Some are tinier than a pinhead. Others are pretty big!

The world's largest land snail is the giant African snail, which grows as large as a rabbit. The biggest one ever recorded, named Gee Geronimo, was caught in Sierra Leone in West Africa in 1976. It measured 15 inches (38 centimeters) long and weighed nearly 2 pounds (0.9 kilograms)—as much as a big bag of flour. Some snails that live in the sea grow even larger than land snails. Giant conch snails can measure 28 inches long (71 centimeters).

Opposite page: *Giant African land snails are the biggest snails in the world. They can be almost 1 foot (30 centimeters) long.*

Snails Everywhere

Snails are found almost everywhere on Earth except the polar regions. On land they mostly live in damp places such as woods and shady meadows. Some live high in trees in tropical rain forests. These moist surroundings help keep their bodies from drying out. However, some types of snails live on bare, rocky mountains. They even live in hot, dry deserts where it hardly ever rains.

Most types of snails live in water. Some live in freshwater ponds, streams, and rivers or mudflats where rivers reach the sea. But over half of all snail species are found in the oceans, as you might guess from all the shells you can find on the seashore. Some cling to sandy or rocky coasts; others slither along in the warm, shallow waters offshore. Some snails creep around in the inky-black, ice-cold ocean depths!

Many snails, like this common pond snail, live in ponds
and streams. Common pond snails can also live on land.

*The tough outer part of this Roman snail's body
has emerged from its shell.*

Snail Bodies

Snails' bodies are very different than our own. You have a skeleton of bones to support and protect your body. Snails are entirely soft and squishy. But they are protected by a tough shell. In between the shell and the soft body is a soft sleeve called the mantle.

A snail's soft body has two main parts: a tougher part that sticks out of the shell and a softer part inside it. The muscular outer body includes the snail's head and its broad foot. The fleshy inner body is coiled to fit inside the shell. This part contains many vital body systems, such as a breathing and digestive system. You may be surprised to learn that a land snail has parts such as a heart, lung, stomach, kidney, and intestine similar to the ones you have. However, it has just one lung and one kidney instead of two like you.

Life-giving Oxygen

Opposite page: *The big hole on this banana slug's head is its breathing hole—just like your nose.*

All animals need a constant supply of oxygen to stay alive. Snails are no different. Land snails have a breathing hole on their right side, near the lip of the shell. You can often see this hole if a snail or slug stretches out its body. This opening leads to a lung, like an air-filled bag, in the mantle just under the shell. Oxygen from the air passes through the thin lining of the lung into blood vessels around it. From the lung the blood carries oxygen around the snail's body.

How do snails that live in water absorb oxygen? Some have lungs like land snails. They come to the surface every now and then to take in air. Other snails live on the seabed and so can't keep visiting the surface. They breathe with the help of gills like fish, which can absorb oxygen from the water.

Getting Around

Snails get around quite well without legs on their broad, flat foot. The foot has bands of muscles that move in ripples. This lifts one part of the body at a time to move it forward. So the snail creeps along. The foot grips amazingly well. That is why snails can climb up the sheer glass walls of an aquarium or over slippery rocks.

Land snails ooze a slippery trail of slime from their foot to help them glide along more easily. You can often see the glistening tracks they leave behind them. The slime allows snails to glide smoothly over rough surfaces without getting hurt. Some sea snails have a broad foot divided into two winglike flaps. The snail swims by slowly waving its "wings" up and down.

At a Snail's Pace

Snails are the slowpokes of the animal
world. They are renowned for the slow pace
at which they go about their business. In fact,
you may have heard someone being scolded
for moving "at a snail's pace." Most snails
cover only about 30 feet (10 meters) per hour.
At that rate it would take a snail five days to
cross San Francisco's Golden Gate Bridge.
And it would take a team of snails creeping
in relay 55 years to cross the United States!

Snails move so slowly partly because their
large, heavy shells weigh them down. Slugs
are a bit more speedy. The banana slug is
one of the world's speediest gastropods. It
has been clocked at speeds of nearly 2 miles
(3 kilometers) an hour! People sometimes
race these slugs for fun.

Sensing the World

Snails have many of the same senses you have, including sight, smell, taste, and touch. They have no ears and so can't hear in the same way you can. But through their skin they can sense vibrations shaking the ground. They can easily detect tramping feet approaching, for example.

A snail has two pairs of tentacles on its head. The shorter pair is used for feeling and also for tasting and smelling. The snail's eyes are set on the tips of the other pair. If a snail senses danger, it pulls in its tentacles until they are just tiny bumps on its head. Like you, snails also have sensors in their skin that detect warmth and pain, and also tell them which way up they are. That can be a help when snails are climbing up plants or walls.

The two long stalks on top of this garden snail's head are not feelers but stalks for its eyes.

Supper Time

The animal kingdom can be divided into two main types of creatures: meat-eaters and plant-eaters. Slugs and snails are mainly plant-eaters. They nibble both green and dying plants, including leaves and flowers. Water snails mainly feed on algae and seaweed. However, snails aren't picky eaters. They also eat fungi, the bodies of dead creatures, and droppings—in fact, anything eatable that comes their way.

To tackle their food, snails have a hard, tonguelike probe called a radula. It is lined with row on row of tiny teeth called denticles. The radula works like a cheese grater, rasping plants off rocks and shredding solid food. Outdoors on a quiet night you may hear the little rasping noise of many snail tongues at work, scraping away at plants!

Opposite page: *Snails don't actually bite bits off the leaves they eat. Instead, they saw away the edges with their sawlike tongue.*

23

Garden Pests

Snails' plant-munching habits make them very unpopular with gardeners. Many a keen gardener has proudly planted out rows of little seedlings raised with care only to find the leafy top nibbled off each one the following day! Slugs are equally destructive, munching prize flowers and fruits and vegetables meant for the table. These mollusks can be quite nimble when they are hungry. They can slide up tall plants to reach tender shoots or shrubs to gnaw the bark.

The giant African snail has a giant appetite to match its size. It originally came from Africa. But it has now spread to many other parts of the world—either by accident or because people have released it in new places for food. In their new homes these snails breed rapidly and eat everything in sight. Unfortunately, they take the food of many local animals. In parts of Southeast Asia this oversized mollusk is now a major pest.

*Plant-eating snails can wreak havoc in gardens,
eating their way through masses of leaves and fruit*

Hunting Mollusks

A few types of snails and slugs are meat-eating predators. Most of these species are armed with sharp teeth or a pointed tongue called a radula that can be used like a spear. Fierce slugs with shells burrow through soil to catch worms. They then harpoon the worms with their radulas. Cone sea snails from the Indian and Pacific Oceans have a poisonous radula they use to spear small fish. People have died after being stung by these dangerous snails.

Some sea snails are parasites, which means they live on or inside the bodies of other creatures. These parasitic sea snails live on sea creatures such as coral and starfish, and feed on them. Snails called oyster drills bore into the shells of other mollusks to feast on the soft flesh inside. Whole colonies of oysters and mussels have been wiped out by these burrowing pests.

Opposite page:
Cone snails have a sting that can kill a person. The sting is on a small, sharp barb that shoots out of the mouth. You can see the mouth just below where the long tube sticks out.

Daily Rhythms

We humans live our lives according to a 24-hour rhythm. We are active during the daytime and catch our beauty sleep at night! Snails also run on a 24-hour clock, but they are active at different times than we are. They are out and about at dusk, dawn, and during the hours of darkness. During the day they rest under stones and fallen leaves or hide in flower pots. Of course, snails don't use a watch. They respond to the changing light levels and have a natural body clock that tells the approximate time of day.

Snails don't like bright sunshine, which is why they hide in the daytime. But they love moisture and often come out to feed after a shower of rain. Snails that dwell on the seashore live their lives according to a different rhythm. They rest and creep around in search of food in time with the rising and falling rhythm of the tides.

Survival Skills

In cool countries snails spend the winter in a deep sleep called hibernation. The weather is too cold for them to be active, and there is little leafy food to eat. They may go to sleep during the first cold snap of fall and only wake up the following spring, when the weather warms again.

Many people like spells of hot, sunny weather, particularly during vacation. Snails hate long dry spells. They retreat into their shells and seal the opening with a plug of slime. They go through the drought in a deep sleep similar to hibernation. They only emerge again when rain falls. In California desert snails have been known to sleep for years during droughts and then become active again. In England a desert snail spent four years glued to a display board in the Natural History Museum in London. Suddenly, a spot of moisture brought the snail back to life again, and it began to crawl around!

Opposite page: *When it is dry, some snails in warm places cluster together and retreat into their shells to avoid drying out.*

Mobile Castle

In the olden days people built castles to protect themselves. But castles don't move, so you had to get to the castle to be safe. A snail, however, takes its "castle" everywhere it goes.

At the first hint of danger the snail pulls its whole body inside its little refuge. It then seals the opening with a lidlike flap called the operculum. Enemies then find it very difficult to get at the soft animal inside. The operculum also helps some sea snails keep moist when stranded out of water between tides.

But if shells are so useful, how do slugs manage without one? Some slugs do have a little shell to protect their back. Others hide from predators by squeezing into narrow crevices. Some sea slugs taste very nasty. These kinds are often brightly colored. Enemies see the colors and leave them alone.

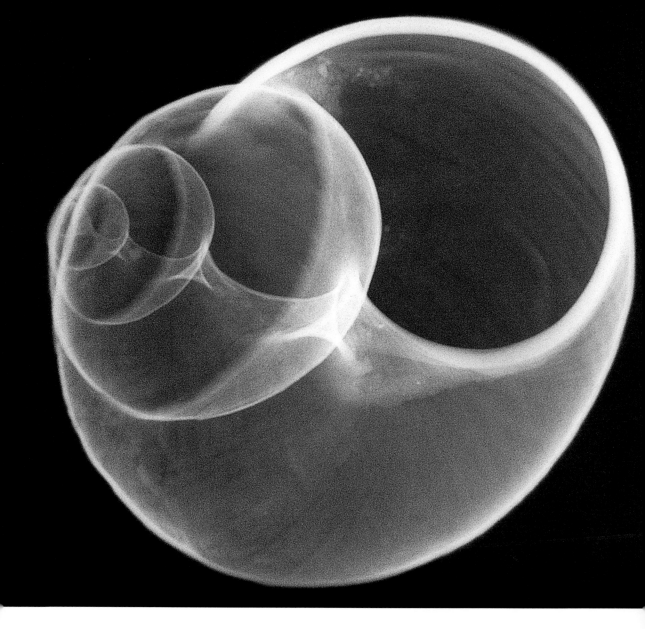

This X-ray image gives a clear picture of the shape of a snail shell on the inside as well as out.

A Natural Marvel

A snail's shell is made from a hard chalky material called calcium carbonate. It oozes out of the snail's mantle as a liquid. It then hardens when touched by water or air.

A snail's shell is a marvel of construction, as you will see if you study one closely. The coiled shape makes it compact—yet it is always roomy enough to fit the snail however big it gets. As a young snail grows up, more shelly material is added to the outer edge of the shell. That way the shell expands to fit the snail's growing body and never gets too tight. Since the shell grows at the outer edge, it builds up in a spiral. So the young snail's first little shell ends up in the center of the spiral. The newest part is the wide mouth—the place where the snail goes in.

The Wonder of Shells

If you have ever collected shells on the shore, you will know that every beach has its own particular mixture of shell species. That is because a huge variety of snails live out at sea. The tides and currents wash different remains ashore on each beach.

The thousands of different types of snail all make shells of a particular shape. Most shells have a spiraling form; but some are shaped like tops, and others like corkscrews, eggs, or barrels. Some shells are brightly striped or patterned. They help disguise the living mollusks against colorful weeds and corals on the seabed. Others are plain, like pebbles. Some shells are shiny; others have a rough surface. Some are smooth, while others are pricklier than a porcupine.

Here are some of the many different–shaped shells found in just a small area of a beach.

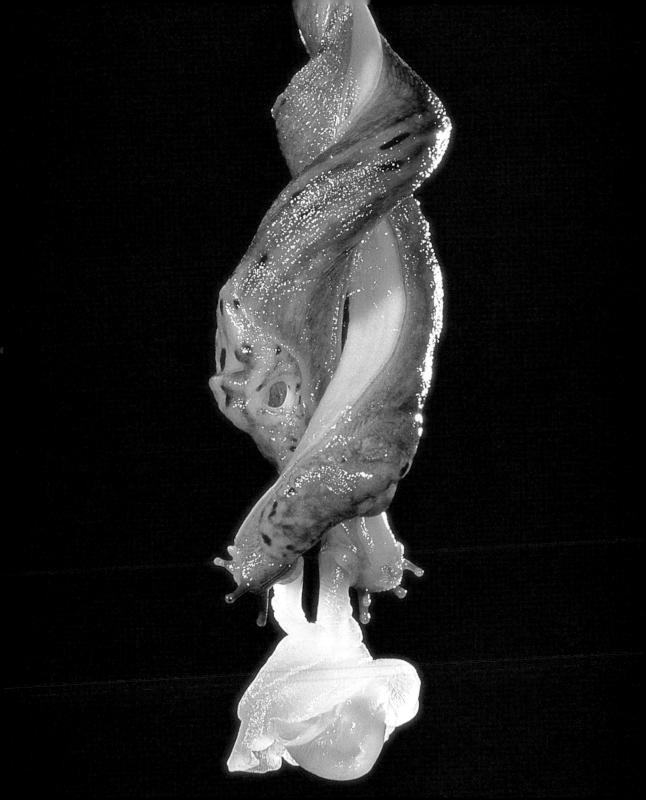

The Mating Game

Most animals are either male or female, and new animals are born after the two mate. A male's body makes a material called sperm that starts a new life when it meets a female's egg. But a snail is both male and female at the same time. That means a single snail can make both sperm *and* eggs. Animals like this are called hermaphrodites (said her-MAFF-row-dites).

Even though a few snails can reproduce by themselves, they still prefer to find a mate. But a mate doesn't have to be a male or a female for some snails, just another snail. That is very useful, because these slow-moving creatures don't bump into one another often.

Many snails court one another for several hours before mating. They do so by twining their bodies together and making a lot of slime. Great gray slugs produce even more slime than most. They crawl up tall plants and then dangle down on a long rope of slime and mate in midair. A few weeks after mating, both mollusks lay eggs.

Opposite page:
To mate, great gray slugs climb a tree. They then twist themselves around each other and dangle down from a thick rope of their own slime, up to 18 inches (46 centimeters) long.

39

Eggs Galore

Almost all snails reproduce by laying small, round eggs. Some are transparent; others have a cloudy shell. The eggs of the giant African snail are the size of a small bird egg. Others are microscopic. Around 80 eggs may be laid at once. Land snails dig a little hollow for their eggs, then fill it with slime and soil. Water snails attach their jelly-coated eggs to stones or seaweed, or carry them around until they hatch.

Most snail eggs are eaten by animals before they get the chance to hatch. Only about five in every 100 eggs survive long enough to become adult snails. The eggs hatch after a few weeks, often in batches of 20 or so at once. They do that because with so many batches, there is less chance all will be eaten by enemies. On land most snail eggs hatch on warm, moist days in summer or fall.

Growing Up

Most young snails hatch as miniversions of their parents. Some sea snails hatch as tiny, free-swimming creatures called larvae. They spend some weeks drifting near the ocean surface. They then sink down to the bottom and begin to grow a shell.

A newborn snail's first action is often to eat its own shell, which is very nourishing. Some snails eat the other eggs that were laid at the same time but have not yet hatched! Snails take between one and four years to grow up. Throughout this time the shell also gets bigger to fit the mollusk's body. When the snail is full-grown, its shell stops growing too. However, the lip, spines, and ridges on the surface go on getting thicker and stronger to give extra protection.

The shells of these young common snails are softer and smoother than those of the adults.

Snail Eaters

Snails have many enemies in the natural world. In the oceans snails are eaten by fish and crabs. On land they are preyed on by birds and a wide range of other animals, including shrews and hedgehogs, frogs, snakes, lizards, and even fierce ground beetles.

A snail's hard shell provides some protection, but birds such as blackbirds can peck open the shells. Some thrushes have learned to smash the shells against stones. You sometimes find these stones, called "anvils," with pieces of shell lying scattered around.

Humans eat snails, too. In France and other countries people enjoy eating garden snails in a dish called escargots (said ESS-car-go) cooked in garlic and butter. People use a special fork to pry the snails out of their shells. People also eat abalone snails from California and the queen conch of the Caribbean. In Australia people use the shiny shells of turban snails to make buttons.

Song thrushes have learned to smash snail shells against stones to get at the soft body inside.

Long Live the Snail!

Around the world some types of snails are at risk of dying out altogether. They are threatened not only by animal predators but also by changes that people have made to the places where they live. One of the world's rarest snails is the Partula snail that lives on islands in the South Pacific ocean. The Partula is now scarce because people brought giant African snails to their islands by accident. The African giant snails bred quickly on the islands. They soon became pests, eating crops. So people brought in a snail that eats snails to control the African giant snails. Unfortunately, the hunting snails preferred to catch the small Partula snails instead. Now the Partula snails are being bred in captivity to try to save them.

Other snails are threatened because the forests, marshes, or grasslands where they live are being cleared for timber or to make way for new towns.

Words to Know

Anvil Flat stone used by a thrush to smash snail shells.

Foot The broad, flat part on which a snail rests, and that contains muscles that allow it to creep along.

Gastropods Group of mollusks that includes slugs and snails.

Hermaphrodite An animal that can make both eggs and sperm.

Larva (plural: **larvae**) A stage in the life of some animals after it hatches, but before it becomes an adult.

Mantle The skin that covers the soft body of a snail, and that also oozes the liquid that makes its shell.

Mollusk A member of the family of soft-bodied animals that includes snails, slugs, clams, mussels, squids, and octopuses.

Operculum The hard patch on a snail's foot that is used to seal the opening of its shell.

Parasite An animal that lives on or inside another animal.

Predator An animal that catches other animals for food.

Radula The long, rough tongue of a snail, which is lined with rows of tiny, horny teeth called denticles.

Species A particular type of animal.

Tentacle One of the four projections on a snail's head that are used to sense its surroundings.

Whorl A spiraling coil on a snail's shell.

INDEX

Cover Photo: Bruce Coleman: Jane Burton
Photo Credits: Ardea: John Daniels 4, 18/19, Steve Hopkin 22, 25, P. Morris 34; Bruce Coleman: Jane Burton 21, John Cancalosi 15; Jeff Jeffords 26; NHPA: Anthony Bannister 29, G.I. Bernard 11, David Middleton 37, Martin Wendler 41, Daniel Zupanc 12; Oxford Scientific Films: Peter Clarke/SAL 45, Paulo Oliveira 42, Rob Nunnington 8, Richard Packwood 38; Still Pictures: Fred Bavendam 7, John Cancalosi 30, Secret Sea Visions 33.